FRIENDLY OFFICERS

By: Miguel Coppedge
Illustrations: Antonio Warrick

Copyright© 2016 Yolanda Coppedge
Illustrated by Antonio Warrick
All rights reserved.

No part of this book may be reproduced in any manner without the written consent of the publisher except for brief excerpts in critical reviews or articles.

ISBN 13: 978-1-61244-499-4
Library of Congress Control Number: 2016913867

Printed in the United States of America

Published by Halo Publishing International
1100 NW Loop 410
Suite 700 - 176
San Antonio, Texas 78213
Toll Free 1-877-705-9647
www.halopublishing.com
www.holapublishing.com
e-mail: contact@halopublishing.com

I dedicate this book to all the police officers who "Protect and Serve" and are involved in their communities. Special dedication to my favorite police officers Bobby Jefferson, Mitch Credle, Natali Thomas, Glay Adams, Kevin Anderson, and Kip Coleman. They are great examples of how ALL police officers should be. I thank you for always supporting me and our communities.

Love,
Miguel

Not all police officers are bad. Most of them do as the oath they took, "Protect and Serve". I want all children to know that they can feel safe regardless of the color of their skin. I'm going to introduce you to my Friendly Officers.

Officer Anderson loves coaching football with the youth every year. He says it brings him joy to serve the youth of his community and for some he serves as a mentor.

Officer Credle helps the youth of his community make short films and teach them how to use their imagination and creativity to change the world.

Officer Jefferson supports young entrepreneurs such as myself and encourages us to be great and stay positive.

Officer Thomas volunteers to read books to children weekly and enjoys it very much!

Officer Coleman loves to play games and have dance offs with the children he comes across daily.

Officer Adams teaches fitness to adults and senior citizens to keep them healthy.

Officer White buys groceries and gifts for families and seniors who can't leave home.

Officer Bill loves talking to homeless people and learning about their life and he also buys them food and find them shelter.

There are a lot of good police in America that treat people with respect and care about the people who live in their communities. Especially children! Police do not want anyone to fear them. There are many "Friendly Officers" of different races like the ones in this story all over the United States that do great things for people of ALL races. We can all get along if we love and respect each other and work together as one.

FRIENDLY OFFICERS QUESTION/ACTIVITY PAGE

Who is your favorite police officer? Why?

What do the police do to help in your community?

Do you feel safe with the police in your community? Why? Why not?

What can police and the community do to help build trust amongst each other?

Draw a picture of how you think the police and communities should work together.

www.ingramcontent.com/pod-product-compliance
Lightning Source LLC
Chambersburg PA
CBHW041439040426
42453CB00021B/2464